Knowing what you BELIEVE

(Christian Doctrines)

Knowing what you believe

(Christian Doctrines)

Prince Mensah

DEDICATION

I dedicate this book to anyone committed to be sound in doctrine and strong in faith.

Table of Contents

1. Introduction to Theology......................1

2. Paterology...7

3. Christology.....................................22

4. Angelology......................................37

5. Anthropology & Hamartiology...............52

6. Soteriology......................................61

7. Bibliology.......................................71

8. Ecclesiology......................................81

9. Eschatology......................................90

10. Contact Information 140

11. Recommendations............................142

Introduction

It's important to know exactly what you believe. There are certain building blocks that are essential beliefs of being a Christian.

It's equally important to search our hearts and figure out what our questions/doubts we have so we can investigate scripture and pray for understanding. As you venture through these lessons I pray you will know, that you know, that you know exactly what you do believe!

If you already serving as a Pastor or Teacher of the word of God for a while, it's always a good thing to revisit some of your most basic beliefs. As we begin to dig into the soil of our faith, we will be taking a good hard look at what we believe. Our spiritual soil should contain truth from scripture so that knowledge and faith grow. With a true and stable foundation in Scripture, our faith will grow in ways only God can imagine.

The quality of our bloom is dependent on the values in our soil but while everyone's soil is specific to himself, the basic foundational beliefs of Christianity are based on the word of God, the Holy Bible.

Acts 17:10-12 *"And the brethren immediately sent away Paul and Silas by night unto Berea: who coming thither went into the synagogue of the Jews. These were more noble than those in Thessalonica, in that they received the word with all readiness of mind, and searched the scriptures daily, whether those things were so. Therefore many of them believed; also of honourable women which were Greeks, and of men, not a few".*

For many years several believers are trapped following blindly whatever someone else said if they thought that person was more "spiritually mature and knowledgeable" than them. But each believer must know the word of God for himself and be like the Thessalonica brethren who goes to cross check the message they were taught.

My point is, how will you know that your spiritual leader(s) are teaching and preaching the true word of God if you don't know God's word? What is the cost of being miss-led spiritually? Who pays the price for any untruths we learn and incorporate into our lives? I can't tell you the number of preachers and speakers I've heard over the years who were speaking values and concepts that were not scripturally based.

Now as a young minister or believer seeking maturity in Christ, it is your responsibility to know the word of God and to preach or teach sound doctrine.

2 Tim 2:2 *"And the things that thou hast heard of me among many witnesses, the same commit thou to faithful men, who shall be able to teach others also."*

This book is to fulfill 2 Tim 2:2 and I believe that as the baton comes to you, you will also be committed to the scripture in raising men and women by the word of God. God bless you.

Chapter 1

Introduction to Theology

The word theology is derived from two Greek words: "theos" which means God and "logos" which means discourse. So therefore theology is the study of God. When used in a broader sense, it can include all the other doctrines revealed in Scripture.

Different Types of Theology

When discussing theology, we must be aware that there are different ways within Christianity of approaching and organizing theology. The most common ones are:

- Natural Theology: Knowledge about God which is derived primarily from nature. Natural theology usually places a heavy emphasis on reason and philosophy. (Psalm 19:1-4)

- Biblical Theology: Knowledge about God which is derived primarily from the Bible. (John 5:39)

- Practical Theology: This focuses on the everyday implications of Christian theological beliefs. This addresses areas such as social justice, church growth and administration, spiritual formation, preaching/homiletics, Christian ethics, Christian family duties, Church duties, and Christian politics. (James 1:22)

- Dogmatic Theology: The word "dogma" comes from a Greek and Latin word meaning "opinion" that is often used alongside theology in reference to official teachings. Therefore, dogmatic theology refers to a set of beliefs officially affirmed by a church body. It focuses on what a particular church body has agreed as what Scripture teaches on a particular issue even though it is not true. (e.g., purgatory, not donating blood, infant baptism, etc.) (Col 2:16)

- Historical Theology: Knowledge about God which is derived from studying the development of ideas over time. (e.g., Theology of the Early Church, Theology of the Imperial Church, Theology of the Middle Ages, Theology of Reformation, etc.) (Joel 1:2-3)

- Systematic Theology: This is the field of study that correlates the data of the Bible as a whole in order to organize the total of God's special revelation. In other words, systematic theology is a way of categorizing what the Bible teaches regarding key areas of the Christian faith such as;

    - Theology Proper (also called Paterology) is the study of what the Bible teaches about God the Father.

    - Christology is the study of God the Son.

    - Pneumatology is the study of God the Holy Spirit.

    - Angelology is the study of angels.

    - Anthropology is the study of

humanity.

- Bibliology is the study of the Bible (also called special revelation).

- Harmartiology is the study of sin.

- Soteriology is the study of salvation.

- Ecclesiology is the study of the Church.

- Eschatology is the study of "last things," including biblical prophecy, the end times, and the afterlife.

You must be sound in doctrine

2 Timothy 3:16 *"All scripture is given by inspiration of God, and is profitable for doctrine, for reproof, for correction, for instruction in righteousness"*

The English word, "doctrine," comes from the Latin word doctrina. It can be defined as, "teaching or instruction." Christian doctrine simply means the beliefs of Christians. A Christian doctrine is what the entire Bible has to say on one particular subject. E.g: "doctrine" of Christ, the "doctrine" of God, the "doctrine" of the church, etc.

Sound doctrine is crucially important that is why Apostle Paul told Titus to *"teach what accords with sound doctrine"* (Titus 2:1). Meaning, Titus's teaching had to correspond with scriptures.

Sound doctrine is important because what we believe affects what we do. There is a direct correlation between what we think and how we act. For example, two people stand on top of a bridge; one believes he can fly, and the other believes he cannot fly. Their next actions will be quite dissimilar. In the same way, a man who believes that there is no such thing as right and wrong will naturally behave differently from a man who believes in well-defined moral standards. In one of the Bible's lists of sins, things like rebellion, murder, lying, and slave trading are mentioned. The list concludes with *"whatever else is contrary to the sound doctrine*" (1 Timothy 1:9-10). In other words, true teaching promotes righteousness; sin flourishes where "the sound doctrine" is opposed.

Sound doctrine is also important because we must ascertain truth in a world of falsehood (false teachers and false prophets). (1 John 4:1)

Sound doctrine is further important because the end of sound doctrine is life while false doctrine leads to death. 1 Timothy 4:16 *"Watch your life and doctrine closely. Persevere in them, because if you do, you will save both yourself and your hearers"*.

Assessment:
- Who is a Theologian? And what kind of theologian are you going to be?
- Why does Christian doctrine cause so much division?
- What is false doctrine?
- What are doctrines of demons, as stated in 1 Timothy 4:1?

Chapter 2

Paterology

This is the study of God the Father in seeking to understand and know Him as a person.

Jeremiah 9:24 *"But let him who glories glory in this, That he understands and knows Me, That I am the LORD, exercising lovingkindness, judgment, and righteousness in the earth. For in these I delight," says the LORD"*.

The Possibility of the Knowledge of God

God is incomprehensible but knowable. Both are true, but not in an absolute sense. Incomprehensible simply means that finite man cannot know everything there is to know about God who is an infinite being. Knowable means man can know God to the needed degree required to trust God and have a personal relationship with Him.

Job 11:7 *"Can you discover the depths of God? Can you discover the limits of the Almighty?"*

John 17:3 *"And this is eternal life, that they may know Thee, the only true God, and Jesus Christ whom Thou hast sent"*.

A healthy relationship with God must begin with an intellectual knowledge of who He is, which then matures into a deeper personal experience of knowing God in life. God manifests Himself to us on the mountain peaks, in the valleys, in the swamps—in all aspects of our lives.

The Existence of God

As a Minister, we know that our sole authority for belief in the existence of God is the inspired and inerrant word of God. Alongside the scriptures, we should be able to explain the existence of God using philosophical and natural means such as;

- It is inexcusable to miss the existence of God from the natural realm. (Rom 1:20)

- Man's wisdom and rational can perceive the existence of God (Psalm 14:1; 53:1)

- Man's conscience and thoughts bears to the existence of God (Rom 2:14-15).

False Views about God

The following are a few of the false views about God. These are either a product of rationalization or the failure of men to accept the Word of God by faith or both.

- Atheism says, "There is no God." They try to explain every phenomenon by mechanical inherent forces saying the universe and all that is in it started by itself, evolved into its present form by itself, and is preserved by itself. (Psalm 14:1; 53:1)

    - The Absolute Atheist: This is one who denies the absolute existence of God.

    - The Providential Atheist: This person simply doubts the existence of God, but firmly denies His providential dealings and the care of God for the things of this world.

- The Practical Atheist: These do not actually deny the being of God, but by their actions and lifestyle communicate otherwise. (Titus 1:16)

- Agnosticism: This theory says there may be a God; but, if there were, He cannot be known. He must forever be the Unknown and the Unknowable.

- Materialism: This is the system which tries to explain everything by physical causes which can be observed and understood. It denies and excludes any spiritual causes.

- Polytheism: This believes in many gods. Most heathenism or most idolatry is a religion of polytheism or "many gods." There are over 300 million gods in India.

- Pantheism: This is the belief that God is in everything and that everything is God. This system confuses God with nature, matter with Spirit, and the creation with the Creator.

- Deism: This view acknowledges that there is a God and that He is the Creator but denies to Him any personal interest or intervention in the world after that. It holds the mechanical self-sustaining theory: God created and then withdrew. He left resident forces, which carry on in His absence.

- Theism: This is the true Bible position. It teaches the existence of God as personal Creator.

- Monotheism: This teaches the singularity of God. (Deut 6:4) Those that hold this believe are; Mohammedans, the Jewish and Christians.

The Nature of God

What's the fundamental nature of God like? How exactly does He exist? Is He personal, or simply an impersonal force? Is He spirit, material, or a combination?

- **The Personality of God**

God, according to the Bible, is both transcendent and immanent.

  - **As Transcendent** God is independent of, above, and distinct from this universe; He is outside, above, and before this time-space universe. (Ex. 3:14) (Psalm 115:3)

  - **As Immanent** God pervades and sustains the universe, yet He is always distinct from it. He is everywhere, yet not in everything. He is personally and intimately involved, yet distinct. (Proverbs 5:21) (Psalm 33:13-14)

Personality is "who I am in the inside and what I do at the outside" which describe and distinguish God, as a person and not a mere force.

  - Self-Consciousness (Ex. 3:14)

  - Intelligence or Thinking Mentality (Ps. 147:5)

  - Self-Determination or Will (Ps. 115:3)

- Sensibility or Emotion (Gen. 6:6) (Prov. 6:16)

- **The Spirituality of God**

God is Spirit (John 4:24). He is without a material body or substance, without physical parts therefore free from all temporal limitations (Luke 24:39), invisible and incorruptible (Col. 1:15; 1 Tim. 1:17).

- **The Trinity (Triunity) of God**

The bible clearly establishes that there is only one God who exists. We find this truth clearly taught in the Old Testaments (Deuteronomy 6:4, 2 Samuel 7:22, Psalm 86:10) and in the New Testament (1 Corinthians 8:4, Galatians 3:20; 1 Timothy 2:5, James 2:19).

However, the bible also taught us that there are three that bear record in heaven; the Father, the Word, and the Holy Ghost: and these three are one (1 John 5:7). Throughout the bible, we can also fine this one God eternally exists in three Persons: the Father, the Word/Son, and the Holy Spirit; and these three are one God, co-equal and co-eternal, having precisely the same nature and attributes, and worthy of precisely the same worship, confidence, and obedience. (Genesis 1:26-27; Matthew 3:16, 17; Matthew 28:19, 20; Mark 12:29; John 1:14; Acts 5:3, 4; 2 Corinthians 13:14)

- **Other nature of God includes;**
  - God is Light (1 John 1:5, 9); God is Love (1 John 4:8) (1 John 2:10); God is a Fire (Heb 12:29) (Deut 4:24) (Isaiah 4:4); etc.

The Attributes (Essence) of God

The attributes of God are the qualities or characteristics inherent in and ascribed to God. These could also be called the "perfections of God" because God is the very essence of the totality of these perfect attributes.

The attributes of God could be defined as, those distinguishing characteristics of the divine nature which are inseparable from the idea of God and which constitute the basis and ground for his various manifestations to his creatures. (A. H. Strong, Systematic Theology (Valley Forge, Pa.: Judson, 1907), p. 244.)

- Classified in two categories:
    - Absolute: incommunicable (Intransitive) (Moral) - Attributes distinct to God alone

    - Relative: communicable (Transitive) (Non-moral)) – Attributes of God that can be found in man albeit in an imperfect and finite resemblance.

- Incommunicable Attributes
    - Self-Existence: This means that God exists independently of any cause. (Ex. 6:3; 3:14).

    - Eternity: It means that the nature of God is without beginning or end, that God is free from all succession of time, and that God contains within Himself the cause of time. (Genesis

21:33) (Psalm 90:1-2)

- Infinite: It means He is without limitations. He has no bounds or limits. He is not limited by the universe nor by time-space boundaries. (1 Kings 8:27) (Acts 17:24-28)

- Immutability: It means God is not subject to change. He is the same yesterday, today, and forever. (Numbers 23:19) (1 Samuel 15:29) (James 1:17)

- Omnipresence: God fills all space and pervades all things with His invisible and immaterial substance while being distinct from all things. (Jer. 23:24)

- Omniscience: This means that God is all knowing. (1 Sam 16:7) (1 Kings 8:39) (Psalm 44:21)

- Omnipotent: This means that God is all powerful. (Gen 17:1) (Job 42:2) (Isaiah 26:4)

- Transcendence: The attributes of God are further manifested in the fact that He is transcendent to the world that means that God is above and beyond His creation (Psa. 139:7-12).

- Sovereignty: As the Lord of creation, God has the absolute right to govern and dispose of the universe as He pleases despite the attempts of man to frustrate His will. (Psa. 50:21) (1 Chronicles 29:11,12) (Daniel 4:35)

- Communicable Attributes
    - Holiness (1 John 1:5) (Revelation 15:4).
    - Righteousness and Justice (Deut. 4:8).
    - Goodness (Exodus 34:6) (Romans 2:4) (1 Timothy 4:4).
    - Mercy (Ex. 33:19).
    - Love (1 John 4:8, 16).

The Names of God

God's names reveal God's attributes, acts, and personal dealings in the world.

1. **Yahweh**: This is the name of God Almighty. It is composed of four Hebrew consonants (YHWH, known as the Tetragrammaton). Ancient Hebrew did not have vowels, so when the Hebrew Bible was first written down in the Hebrew language, they wrote only with consonants "YHWH". (Exodus 3:13-14) (Deut 6:4) (Daniel 9:14)

The meaning of the name 'Yahweh' has been interpreted as "He Who Makes That Which Has Been Made" or "He Brings into Existence Whatever Exists". This particular name was so sacred to the Jewish scribes that when they would come to this name, they would stop and make themselves ceremonial clean. This name is so sacred that they substitute with Adonai (Lord) or Elohim (supreme one) for fear of taking His name in vain but as a result, the pronunciation was lost, and neither Jewish nor Christian scholars are sure how it was pronounced.

In the 6th through 10th centuries, the Masoretes, who worked to reproduce the original Hebrew text of the Bible, inserted the vowels from Adonai or Elohim into YHWH to get YeHoWeh or YeHoWaH. However, "Y" doesn't exist in Latin, so Latin-speaking Christian scholars replaced the "Y" with "J" to get "JeHoWaH," which became "Jehovah" as it spread throughout medieval Europe.

2. **Elohim**: The plural form of EL, meaning "strong one." Is used of false gods, but when used of the true God, it is a plural of majesty and intimates the trinity. Is especially used of God's sovereignty, creative work, mighty work for Israel and in relation to His sovereignty (Gen. 1:1) (Isa. 54:5) (Jer. 32:27)

3. **Adonai**—Lord, Master; Most common name when Yahweh thought to be too sacred to pronounce (Ex 4:10-12)

4. Compounds of El:
   - El Shaddai: "God Almighty" (Gen. 17:1) (Ex. 6:31) (Psalm 91:1, 2).

   - El Elyon: "The Most High God."

Stresses God's strength, sovereignty, and supremacy (Gen. 14:19) (Psalm 9:2).

- El Olam: "The Everlasting God." Emphasizes God's unchangeableness (Gen. 16:13).

- El HaKadosh - The Holy God (Isa 5:16)

- El HaNeeman - The Faithful God (Deut 7:9)

5. Compounds of Yahweh (Jehovah):
   - Yahweh Jireh (Yireh): "The Lord will provide." (Gen. 22:14).

   - Yahweh Nissi: "The Lord is my Banner." (Ex. 17:15).

   - Yahweh Shalom: "The Lord is Peace." (Jud. 6:24).

   - Yahweh Sabbaoth: "The Lord of Hosts." (1 Sam. 1:3; 17:45).

- Yahweh Maccaddeshcem: "The Lord your Sanctifier." (Ex. 31:13).

- Yahweh Roi: "The Lord my Shepherd." (Ps. 23:1).

- Yahweh Tsidkenu: "The Lord our Righteousness." (Jer. 23:6).

- Yahweh Shammah: "The Lord is there." (Ezek. 48:35).

- Yahweh Elohim Israel: "The Lord, the God of Israel." (Jud. 5:3; Isa. 17:6).

Assessment: How does your understanding of the Trinity and God's will influence your daily life? Specifically meditate on each: Father, Son, Holy Spirit.

Chapter 3

Christology

Christology is the area of theology that discusses issues related to Jesus pre-existence, His deity and humanity, His earthly birth, life, death, resurrection, ascension, future return, and eternal reign.

The Pre-Existence of Christ

Indeed our Lord Jesus Christ existed as the second person in the Godhead trinity from the beginning before He became flesh on earth. Those who deny to Jesus Christ pre-existence to His birth at Bethlehem are those who deny His possession of more than a human nature. However, let us take a look at the proofs of Jesus' pre-existence.

- The testimony of Jesus Himself
  - His Oneness with the Father, (John10:30), signifying a co-existence with God.

- His existence before Abraham (John 8:58).

- He claim about the Father loving him from eternity past (John 17:24) (John.13:3)

- His glory before the world was formed (John17:5)

- The Testimony of the Prophets.
  - Micah 5:2; Isaiah 7:14; 9:6-7.

  - John the Baptist. John 1:30 - "He is preferred before me; for He was before me." Yet from Luke 1:26 we find out that, naturally speaking, John the Baptist was six months older than Jesus. He could only have reference to Christ's pre-existence.

- The Testimony of the Apostles
  - John – John 1:1-5, 14.

- Paul - Philippians 2:6, I Timothy 3:16, Colossians 1:15-16.

- The Book of Hebrews. 1:2- 3; 13:8

- The Testimony of Implication.
    - The works of creation are ascribed to Christ - (John 1:3); Colossians 1:16; Hebrews 1:10.

    - The many titles of Deity ascribed to Christ relate Him to the Jehovah of the Old Testament; therefore, eternally existing. "The Son of God," "First and Last," "Alpha and Omega," "The Lord," "Lord of All," "The Mighty God," "Everlasting Father," "God with us." See how Jesus Himself uses this to affirm His Deity and answer the question of His Sonship. Matthew 22:42-45.

    - His pre-existence is implied by the fact that He is to be worshipped as God. John 20:28; Hebrews 1:6 - Worship of the Angels given Him.

The Incarnation

The word "Incarnate" literally from the Latin means, "Enfleshment," the taking of humanity.

How plainly that fact of Christ's Enfleshment is seen in Hebrews 2:14. So therefore, let us not that the only Redeemer of God's elect is the Lord Jesus Christ, who being the eternal Son of God, became man, and so was, and continues to be, God and man, in two distinct natures, and one person forever. Christ the Son of God, became man, by taking to himself a true body and a reasonable soul, being conceived by the power of the Holy Ghost, in the womb of the Virgin Mary, and born of her, yet without sin. Christ is the Messiah which was to come. The promised Seed of the woman (but not of the man) was fulfilled in the virgin birth (Gen. 3:15).

- The **True Humanity of Christ**: There are simple proofs of this Humanity - such as, His natural birth, His natural life with human frailties and feelings, of hunger, thirst, weariness, temptation, suffering, weeping, sorrowing, and death. These belong primarily to human beings. God cannot be tempted nor experience any of these other sensations; neither can He be touched with death. He Himself told Thomas, "Handle Me and see, for spirit hath not flesh and bones as ye see Me have." (Luke 24:39) (Rom 1:3) (Heb 2:14)

- **The Personality of Christ:** In addition to being God incarnate, the Scriptures reveal that Jesus had a human soul with its powers of intellect, feeling, will and conscience. The Lord loved, sympathized, wept, exercised the feelings of a man, thought, talked, willed, made choices, groaned in spirit, and was troubled. (Heb 2:16-17) (Luke 2:52) (Matt 26:38) If Jesus did not have a human soul as well as a human body, He would not be truly man.

- **Errors as to the person of Christ: Denial of His Humanity**

The Gnostics denied Christ's humanity on the ground of their Manichaean philosophy that taught that evil arises from matter. Man consists of a spirit combined with a material body and this union with the material defiles the spirit. Salvation therefore consists in emancipation from the body. To effect this redemption Christ came into the world. It was necessary He should appear as a man; but as He could not be connected with matter and retain His spirituality His body was only a phantasm, a mere appearance without substance or reality. He therefore was not born nor did He suffer and die. Some admitted he had a body not of matter but some ethereal or celestial substance.

The Deity of Christ

Jesus is God, the second person of the Trinity. This is proven in several ways.

- Jesus Claimed to be divine (John 6:38) (John 8:42, 58) (John 10:38) (John 14:9-10)

- The Apostles taught that Jesus was divine (Matt 1:23; 16:26) (Mark 1:1) (John 1:1, 14) (Col 1:16)

- The confession of others concerning Christ's deity (Isaiah 9:6) (Matt 27:54) (Luke 4:41)

- The sacred title of God applied to Christ prove His Divinity
    - Jesus is called Emmanuel Matt. 1:23
    - Jesus is called God John 20:28
    - Jesus is called the Alpha and Omega Rev. 1:11
    - Jesus is called the King of kings and Lord of lords 1 Tim. 6:15

- The Authority that has Been Entrusted to Christ Proves His Deity (John 5:22) (Acts 10:42) (Acts 17:31)

- The attributes of Deity are ascribed to Him.
    - Omnipresent (Matt 28:20)
    - Omniscience (I Cor 4:5; Col 2:3)
    - Omnipotent (Matt 28:18)
    - Self-existence (John5:26)

- Immutability (Heb 13:8)
- Life (John 1:4)

- **Errors as to the Deity of Christ: Denial of His Humanity and Denial of His Divinity.**

  - **The Arians** (followers of Arius, a presbyter in Alexander, Egypt, AD 320) held that God was one eternal person and that Christ was the first created being, by whom God created the world, super-angelic, became incarnate in Jesus of Nazareth. Nevertheless, He was a creature of different substance from God (Gk. *heter-oousios*). The Semi-Arians held that the absolute self-existent God was one person. The Son was a Divine Person, not equal with the Father, not identical in substance, but similar (Gk. *homo-i-ousios*). Unitarians now deny the Deity of Christ. They consider Him a mere man.

- **The Apollinarians** (followers of Apollinaris of Laodicea, AD 390) held that Jesus Christ had a human body and a human soul but no human mind or spirit. The Logos replaced these things. This position was embraced because of a belief that *every* man's soul was part of the Divine substance. They therefore attacked the two complete natures in Christ.

- **The Nestorians** denied the union of the two natures in one person. They insisted on the distinction of the two natures till they practically made two persons. In AD 428 Nestorius was appointed Bishop of Constantinople. Wanted to purify his diocese of any hint of unorthodoxy, he attacked the popular veneration being given to the Virgin Mary while trying to reassure the followers of Mohammed that Christianity taught the worship of one God. His teachings led to the conclusion that the human Jesus could not be worshiped and that unity of Christ's person between the mortal and the immortal, the flesh and the Divine was merely a union of the will rather than a true hypostatic union. Opposed by Cyril of Alexandria, Nestorius was deposed at the Council of Ephesus in AD 431 and exiled in AD 436.

- **The Eutychians** (fifth century AD) went to the opposite extreme and said there was only one nature and that was Divine. Everything about Christ was Divine, even His body was Divine. According to Eutyches, living in a monastery outside Constantinople, it was the Logos that was born, and the Logos that suffered and died. Eutyches said that there were two natures before the union, but only one after the Incarnation. The two natures of Christ were so unified as to become one.

- **The Doctrine of Kenosis:** This important doctrine is based upon the

Greek word for "emptying" in Philippians 2:7. This view teaches that the Logos became man by reducing Himself to the capacity of a babe and increased in wisdom and power till at length He assumed Divine nature much like the flame in a gas heater can be started by a small spark and then turned up.

- **The Socinians** held that Christ was a mere man in Himself, had no prior existence but had a miraculous birth, and was baptized with the Holy Ghost and became Divine and is to be worshipped.

- **The Jehovah Witnesses** reflect more modern deniers of the deity of Christ. They believe that Christ was a man on earth but became God. Since Christ was called God while on earth and claimed to be God while on earth and was called Son of God before He was born, this means that this doctrine is error.

The works of Christ

- **The Mediatorial Office of Christ**

  - **Prophet** (Christ is the revealer of God who represent God before man);
    - ➤ Christ revealed God in the Old Testament.
    - ➤ Christ revealed God by the inspiration of the prophets.
    - ➤ Christ revealed God through the Incarnation, with its direct and personal teachings, *"I speak that which I have seen."*
    - ➤ Christ is the completed revelation of God (Rev. 22:18).
    - ➤ Christ reveals God by being a spokesman of God

  - **Priest** (He represent man before God);
    - ➤ What is a priest? (Heb 5:1) (Heb 8:3). As every high priest is ordained to offer gifts and sacrifices therefore it is needful that this one also have something to offer. In the Old Testament the priest offered

expiatory sacrifice on the ground of which men's sins were remitted.

- ➤ He came to God for men, presented sacrifices and interceded for them. He was thus a mediator between God and man.
- ➤ The Old Testament priesthood was a type of Christ's priesthood. The priesthood was fulfilled in Christ. There is now no priest in the strict sense of that word. There is no expiatory sacrifice now to be offered. Christ did that once for all.

- **King** (Christ came as King);
  - ➤ God as Creator was and is sovereign over all His creatures.
  - ➤ He is the king of the Jew (Mark 15:2)
  - ➤ Jesus rules and reign and has all authority in heaven and on earth and under the earth both the spiritual or physical, visible or

invisible above all government and name or titles. (Eph 1:20-22)

> In future Christ will rule and reign with the redeemed. This is known as the millennial reign (Rev 12:10)

- **Christ (Messiah);** Jesus alone is the "Anointed One" He was anointed by the Holy Spirit and did the messianic task. (Matt 3:16) (Luke 4:18) (Acts 10:38)

- **Savior;** Our Lord Jesus was sent into this world to be our savior. (1 John 4:14) (Matt 1:21)

- **Redeemer;** Jesus came to redeem us from;
    - The curse of the Law (Gal 5:13)
    - Satan (Heb 2:15)
    - A sinful life style (1 Peter 1:18)
    - A fallen kingdom (Gal 1:4)

- **Lord**; Jesus is sovereign and master of all creation (Phil 2:9-11) (Acts 2:36)

- **Baptizer**; Jesus baptize us with His Spirit (John 1:33; 16:7)

Assessment:

1. Why is Christ's death also the central fact of Christianity?

2. How can you know that the resurrection is fact, not fiction?

3. Assume that you have a non-Christian friend who asks you, "Who is Jesus? Why should I believe in him?" How would you respond, based on the information in this lesson?

Chapter 4

Angelology

Are you aware that angels appear in the Bible from the beginning to the end, from the Book of Genesis to the Book of Revelation?

Did you know that angels are mentioned about 273 times in the entire bible and more than 165 times in the New Testament alone?

Do you know that even though each believer has angels that ministers to him or her regularly, every prophet or prophetic minister has increase angelic activities around him or her lives?

One of the greatest benefits God has given His church and prophets is angelic assistance. Understanding their role and knowing how to minister with them under the supervision of the Holy Spirit will take your prophetic ministry to the next level.

Revelation 19:10 *"And I fell at his feet to worship him* [an angel]. *But he said to me, "See that you do not do that! I am your fellow servant, and of your brethren who have the testimony of Jesus. Worship God! For the* *testimony of Jesus is the spirit of prophecy."*

The reality of Angels

Angels are real and the Bible establishes beyond all doubt the reality of angels.

1. When we examine the **Old Testament**, for example, we find that angels are mentioned 108 times.

   - Angels intervened in the lives of the patriarchs Abraham and Jacob, as indicated in the Book of Genesis (chaps. 18,19,28,32).

   - Moses also knew the ministry of angels in his life, both in his call to return to Egypt (Ex. 3:2) and during the wilderness wanderings (Ex. 14:19). In all, the word *angel* or *angels* appears in the books of the Law, the writings of Moses, a total of 32 times.

   - Turn to the books of history and read of angelic activity in Joshua, Judges, 1 and 2 Samuel, 2 Kings, and in 1 and 2 Chronicles. Some 37 references to the work and ministry of angels relate to the development of the kingdom of Israel.

- Those who wrote the books of poetry continued to unfold the existence of angels.

- The oldest book of the Bible, Job, speaks of angels (e.g., 4:18).

- Frequently the Psalms describe angels as protecting and delivering God's people from all kinds of danger (e.g., 34:7; 91:11).

- With the exception of Jeremiah, all the **major prophets** alluded to the ministry of angels.

- Of the **minor prophets**, Hosea and Zechariah speak of angels.

2. The **New Testament** continues to enlarge our knowledge of angelic beings.

- The gospels are filled with references to them from announcing the birth of John the Baptist and Jesus, to ministering songs, giving direction for escape, ministering to Jesus, passing message to disciples, etc.

- Six times in the Book of Acts, angels ministered to the Lord's people (e.g., 5:18-20).

- The writer of half the epistles, Paul, spoke of angels in many of the books that bear his name.

- James and Peter spoke of angels in their letters.

- The book of Revelation, refers to angels no fewer than 65 times.

3. Finally the **testimony of the Lord Jesus Christ** also proves the reality of angels as he spoke of angels some couple of times during his earthly.

So we know with absolute certainty from the Bible and from the Son of God that angels are real.

Descriptions of Angels

The Greek word ἄγγελος or "angelos" means messenger or angel. Angels are the heavenly messengers of God, often delivering God's message and carry out God's commands.

1. Their Nature and Attributes...

- They are spirit beings
  - Called "spirits", suggesting they do not have corporeal bodies - Heb 1:14
  - They are invisible to the human eye but are revealed at times
  - They can reveal themselves at times in human form - Gen 18:3
  - They do not function as human beings in such things as marriage - Mark 12:25
  - They are not subject to death - Luke 20:36

- They are created beings
  - They are part of the creation that is to praise Jehovah - Psalm 148:1-5
  - They were created by Christ, among all other things - Col 1:16

- They are innumerable
  - An innumerable company - Heb 12:22

- - John's descriptions suggests their number is countless - Rev 5:11

- They are a higher order than man
  - - Man was created lower than the angels - Heb 2:6-7
  - - Angels are not capable of death - Luke 20:36
  - - They have greater wisdom, though limited - 2 Sam 14:20; Matt 24:36
  - - They have greater power, though it too is limited - Matt 28:2; Dan 10:13

- They always appeared as men
  - - Never as women or children, always clothed
  - - Other than Cherubim and Seraphim (whose classification as angels is suspect), they never have wings – though. Rev 8:13; 14:6
  - - Many times they were so disguised as men, they were not first identified as angels – Gen 18:1-2; 19:1; Heb 13:2

2. Hierarchy of Angels – Names and ranks

In the military, all personnel are ranked whether enlisted men or officers. In the Ghana army, for example, we have the Field Marshal at the top and then down through General, Lieutenant General, Major General, Brigadier, Colonel, Major, Captain, Lieutenant And 2nd Lieutenant. And enlisted men also are ranked from Warrant office 1, Warrant office 2, Staff Sergeant, Sergeant, Corporal, Lance Corporal and Private.

Just like the military, angels are ranked. Let's take a look at the hierarchy of angels ranked from the highest to lowest;

- **Jesus Christ**, though not an angel, He is the Commandant of the Heavenly Host. (Joshua 5:13-15) (Eph 1:21)

- **Seraphim** are the highest order of the Hierarchy of Angels aside the Lord.

    - Sometimes called "the burning ones" because they are closest to God and radiate pure light.

- Six winged creatures attending the Lord in Isaiah's vision - Isa 6:1-13

- Their description is also akin to those of the four living creatures in Revelation rather than angels - cf. Rev 4:8-9

- These angelic beings spend their time worshiping and praising God.

- The prophet Isaiah vividly describes them in his vision of God: He quotes in Isaiah 6:1-3 *"In the year that King Uzziah died, I saw the Lord sitting on a throne, high and lifted up, and the train of His robe filled the temple. Above it stood seraphim; each one had six wings: with two he covered his face, with two he covered his feet, and with two he flew. And one cried to another and said: 'Holy, holy, holy is the Lord of hosts; the whole earth is full of His glory".*

- **Cherubim** are the second highest order after Seraphim.
    - The Bible depicts Cherubim as the bearers of God's Throne, as the charioteers, and as powerful beings with four wings and four faces. (Ezekiel 1 :5 – 1 4; 28: 1 2)

    - They are also depicted on the Ark of the Covenant as its Guardians.

    - God sent them to guard the gate of Eden after the expulsion of Adam and Eve (Genesis 3:23-24)

- **Thrones** are the third ranking order of angels (Colo 1:16) (Daniel 7:9)
    - They are called the 'many eyed ones'
    - They have the duty of carrying out God's decisions.
    - They are often represented as firey wheels.

- **Dominions** are the fourth ranking order of angels (Colo 1:16)

- Their job is to regulate the duties of the other angels and ensure that God's wishes are carried out.

- According to Jewish traditions, the success or failure of nations was decided by this Order of Guardian Angels. Dominations have been described as wearing long albs, or gowns reaching to their feet, hitched with a golden belt and adorned with a green sole. They carry golden staffs in the right hand and the Seal of God in the left. At other times, they are said to hold an orb or a specter.

- **Principalities or Princes** are the fifth ranking order of angels. (Colo 1:16)

  - The Principalities were considered to be the guardians over the nations and the leaders of the world.

  - It is believed that they are given more freedom to act than the lesser angels below them.

- They are directly involved in human affairs and serve to protect man and convey the Word of God.

- They are responsible for carrying out divine acts concerning their area of jurisdiction.

- They are given to the task of managing the duties of the angels.

- Principalities have been described as being dressed in soldier's uniforms with golden girdles.

- **Powers** are the sixth ranking order of angels. (Colo 1:16)
  - Their job is to prevent the 'fallen angels' from taking over the world and keeping the Universe in balance.

  - They are also seen as the Angels of birth and death.

- **Archangels** are seven ranking order of angels.
  - Archangels also are directly involved in human affairs and serve to protect man and convey the Word of God.

- Archangel Michael is believed to be the highest ranking war angel in God's heavenly host. (Dan 12:1) (Dan 10:13) (Jude 1:6) (Rev 12: 79)

- Archangel Gabriel is a highest ranking messenger angel who brought special messages to God's people. In the Scripture we find him bringing messages to:
  - ➢ Daniel to reveal the future events to him (Daniel 8:16; 9:21).
  - ➢ He went to Zacharias regarding the birth of John the Baptist, (Luke 1 :19)
  - ➢ To Mary to announce the birth of Jesus (Luke 1:30)

- According to Jewish tradition (but not the Bible – we are given the Bible to live by not any other books) the seven archangels are;
  - ➢ Michael
  - ➢ Gabriel
  - ➢ Raphael (Book of Tobit 12:15) - Healing angel
  - ➢ Uriel

> ➤ Raguel
> ➤ Saraqael
> ➤ Remiel

- **Holy Ones and Watchers** are the eight ranking order of angels. (Dan 4:13,17,23)
    - These angles know times, seasons and cycles of the Lord. As time keepers, they observe and monitor events that take place on the earth and the activities of God's people and how they respond to fulfill their destiny.

    - They announced judgment (Dan 4:17).

    - They watch over the degrees of the Lord and enforces it on earth (Psalm 103:20-21)

    - So whenever the words are spoken by the Spirit of prophecy these angels see to it that the word comes to pass in the lives of those that will respond to the word of God under the approval of God.

- They may also be assigned to the sons of Issachar (1 Chron 12:32)

- **Heavenly host/ Angels** are the last order of angels.
    - They are believed to be ministering angels sent forth to minister for those who will inherit salvation (Hebrews 1:14).

    - Within the orders of angels, only archangels and angels (the lowest categories in the hierarchy) are traditionally said to interact with man and woman in the course of daily life.

    - In some cases, the angel serves only as a messenger, but in others, the angel lingers in visible form, taking responsibility for the well-being of individuals in trouble, guarding them from harm, offering them sustenance, or leading them out of danger.

    - They are often called "Guardian Angels."

What Angels Do

- God's angels are active and function as the Lord command them.

Class discussion: What do angels do? What are their job descriptions? (10mins discussion and presentation)

Chapter 5

Anthropology & Hamartiology

Anthropology is a word derived from the Greek words (*anthropos* means man, and logos means discourse). We use the word "anthropology" to refer to the study of man and a Biblical anthropology is the study of man as understood primarily from Scripture. Thus it often involves discussion of the particular creation of man, man in the "image of God," the constitutional nature of man, and man after the fall.

Hamartiology, on the other hand, comes from two Greek words (hamartia means "sin" and logos means discourse). Thus it concerns the biblical doctrine of sin including its origin, nature, transmission, effects, and judgment.

The Creation of Man

There are several points that can be made from the Genesis narrative regarding the creation of man (Gen 1-2).

1. The origin of man is not in naturalistic

evolution, but in the mind of God. Man was not an afterthought of some kind, or the result of blind evolutionary forces, but was created according to the purpose, plan, and good pleasure of God. In Genesis 1:26 God says *"let us make man...."*

2. Man has a certain place as the pinnacle of creation. We are made in the "image" of God. Nothing else, including the angels, is said to be made in the image of God. Thus we are, in this sense, unique in the created order, with the result that we are both privileged and responsible (Gen 3).

3. Man bears a special relationship to God. In our original creation, coming from the hand of God, we were holy, upright, and perfect and there was no hostility between God and us.

4. Man has a certain role in creation. We were created to rule over God's created earth, that is, to have dominion over it.

5. Man was created in what appears as an instantaneous act of God, bringing together material aspects and "the breath of life." According to Genesis 2:7, our creation gives rise to the dual nature of our experience as we relate in both a heavenward (spiritual) and earthward (material) direction.

The Constitutional Nature of Man

- Man as created generally with both material and immaterial substances. The dust of the earth and the breath of God.

  - Dichotomy theory: According to Genesis 2:7, man is composed of only two substances, the body and the soul. The body is material substance; the soul is immaterial substance. (Matthew 10:28) (1 Kings 17:21)

  - Trichotomy theory: This is of the view that man is composed of three substances: body, soul, and spirit. (1 Thessalonians 5:23) (Hebrews 4:12) The body being material substance and the spirit and soul are the immaterial substance.

- Arguments against the Trichotomous Theory
    - The Scriptures use the terms soul and spirit interchangeably. (Job 32:8) (John 13:21)

The Fall of Man

Genesis 3 describes saddest event in human history where Adam and Eve ignored God's specific command and ate the forbidden fruit leading them to fell from grace. (Gen 2:16-17) the fall of man comprises of the action of three beings namely;

- The Serpent: Satan came into the garden in a form of a serpent to deceive, trick and tempt Eve. (2 Cor 11:3)

- Eve:
    - She was completely deceived by the devil (I Tim 2:14)

- ■ She was tempted in a three-fold guise. (I John 2:16)
  - ➢ Eve saw that the fruit was good for food - "Lust of the flesh".
  - ➢ She saw that the fruit was pleasant to the eyes - "Lust of the eyes".
  - ➢ She very much desired what would make one wise - "Pride of life".

- • Adam: He was not deceived by the devil but willfully transgressed because of his love for the woman. He didn't want to be separated from her. (I Tim 2:14)

The Doctrine of Sin

Romans 5:12 *"Wherefore, as by one man sin entered into the world, and death by sin; and so death passed upon all men, for that all have sinned"*

Basically, sin is a transgression of law (1 John 3:4) and rebellion against God. (Deuteronomy 9:7; Joshua 1:18).

- Sin had its beginning with Lucifer. He was the first to sin and was cast down to earth. He sinned by being prideful which led to his rebellion in heaven. (Isaiah 14:12-15) (Ezekiel 28:12-18) (Revelation 12:1-13). So through Lucifer, sin was created and through his temptation, it was released to man.

- Sin affected the human race by one man, Adam. (Rom 5:12) Since Adam and Eve's rebellion against God and against His command, sin has been passed down through all the generations of mankind. When Adam sinned, his inner nature was transformed by his sin of rebellion, bringing to him spiritual death and depravity which is then passed on to all who came after him. Making anyone who is conceived sinful even before delivery. This passed-on depravity is known as **inherited sin or original sin**. So man becomes a sinner not because he sins but because he carries the nature of sin and hence commits sin. (Psalm 51:5)

- Another type of sin is known as **imputed**

sin. The Greek word translated "imputed" means "to take something that belongs to someone and credit it to another's account." Before the Law of Moses was given, sin was not imputed to man, although men were still sinners because of inherited sin. After the Law was given, sins committed in violation of the Law were imputed (accounted) to them (Romans 5:13).

- **Personal sins** are sins that are committed every day by every human being because of the inherited sinful nature from Adam. These include faithlessness, causing others to sin, hardness of heart against God word, disobedience to God's will and word, etc.

The consequences of Sin

The consequences of sin are doubtless more numerous than we will attempt to consider in this brief study. Below are few;

- Death: For the wages of sin is death (Rom 6:23) (Rom. 1:32). Death is primarily the separation of the soul from God (spiritual death), from body (physical death), from God eternally (eternal death - 2 Thess 1:8-9; Rev 20:15; 21:8).

- The Four-Fold Judgment for Man's Sin
    - The judgment upon the serpent, called in theology, "the curse of degradation." Curse above every beast of the field, the changing of the serpent from upright to crawling position, eating of dust, enmity with the woman, and between their seeds, it's head to be crashed by man (Genesis 3:15)

    - The judgment upon the woman; pain in pregnancy and delivery, husband ruling over her. (Genesis 3:16)

    - The judgment upon the man is sorrow and toil. (Genesis 3:17)

    - The curse upon the ground is; barrenness, thorns, and thistles.

- It breaks fellowship with God (Isaiah 59:1-2)

- It breaks the hedge of God protection over us (Eccl 10:8) (John 14:30) (Eph 4:27)

- Puts man under slavery (John 8:34)

- It affects our heavenly rewards (2 Cor 5:10)

Assessment:
1. Why did God create man?

2. God said in Gen 1:27 that let's man be created in His divine image. Explain the image of God in man.

3. How would you define the term "total depravity"?

Chapter 6

Soteriology

Soteriology, (soteria, salvation, logos, discourse) refers to the study of the doctrine concerning salvation.

The Meaning and Scope of Salvation

According to the broadest meaning as used in Scripture, the term salvation encompasses the total work of God by which He seeks to rescue man from the ruin, doom and power of sin and bestows upon man the wealth of His grace encompassing eternal life, provision for abundant life now, and eternal glory (Eph. 1:3-8; 2:4-10; 1 Pet. 1:3-5; John 3:16, 36; 10:10).

The word "salvation" is the translation of the Greek word soteria which is derived from the word soter meaning "savior." The word "salvation" communicates the thought of deliverance, safety, preservation, soundness, restoration, and healing.

In theology, however, its major use is to denote

a work of God on behalf of men, and as such it is a major doctrine of the Bible which includes redemption, reconciliation, propitiation, conviction, repentance, faith, regeneration, forgiveness, justification, sanctification, preservation, and glorification.

The Motivations for Salvation

When we look at the stubbornness and rebellion of man, we ask the question, why should God want to save sinners? And especially, why should He give His unique and beloved Son to die the agony of God's holy judgment in bearing our sin on the cross?

Scripture's answer is that salvation redounds to the glory of His grace. Here are some of the reasons for salvation:

1. It reveals God's love for man. (John 3:16; 1 John 4:7-10, 16).

2. It's a manifestation of God's grace (Eph. 2:7-9).

3. It manifests the holiness of God.

4. To restore fellowship with man

The Three Phases (Tenses) of Salvation

Salvation in Christ, which begins in eternity past according to the predetermined plan of God and extends into the eternal future, has three observable phases in the Bible.

- **Phase I**: This is the past tense of salvation—saved from sin's penalty. Several passages of Scripture speak of salvation as wholly past, or as accomplished and completed for the one who has believed in the person and work of Jesus Christ. This aspect views the believer as delivered once and for all from sin's penalty and spiritual death (Luke 7:50; 1 Cor. 1:18; 2 Cor. 2:15; Eph. 2:5, 8; Tit. 3:5; Heb. 7:25; 2 Tim. 1:9). So complete and perfect is this work of God in Christ that the believer is declared permanently saved and safe forever (John 5:24; 10:28, 29; Rom. 8:1, 37-39; 1 Pet. 1:3-5).

- **Phase II**: This is the present tense of salvation and has to do with present deliverance over the reigning power of sin or the carnal nature's power in the lives of believers (Rom. 6:1-23; 8:2; 2 Cor. 3:18; Gal. 2:19-20; 5:1-26; Phil. 1:19; 2:12-13; 2 Thess. 2:13). This phase of salvation in Christ is accomplished through the ministry of the indwelling Spirit, but it is based on the work of Christ and the believer's union and co-identification with Christ in that work.

- **Phase III**: This is the future tense of salvation which refers to the future deliverance all believers in Christ will experience through a glorified resurrected body. It contemplates that, though once and for all saved from the penalty of sin and while now being delivered from the power of sin, the believer in Christ will yet be saved into full conformity to Jesus Christ (Rom. 8:29; 13:11; 1 Pet. 1:5; 1 John 3:2). This recognizes and shows that the Christian in his experience never becomes perfect in this life (Phil. 3:12-14). Full conformity to the character of Christ, experientially speaking, awaits ultimate glorification. However, the fact that some aspects of salvation for the one who believes are yet to be accomplished in no way implies that there is ground for doubt as to the outcome of eternal salvation because all three phases are dependent upon the merit and the work of God in His Son, the Lord Jesus Christ.

The Nature of Salvation as the Work of God

Salvation is the free gift of God to man by grace through faith, completely aside from human works.

Works in the life of a believer are tremendously important, but they are to be the result of receiving and appropriating God's grace in the salvation they receive. As the prophet declares, *"Salvation is of the Lord"* (Jonah 2:9).

This saving work of God encompasses various aspects which together accomplish salvation: these include redemption, forgiveness, reconciliation, propitiation, justification, imputation, regeneration, expiation, sanctification, and even glorification. It is all of this and much more which provide salvation, make believers qualified for heaven and become the children of God (John 1:12; Col. 1:12; Eph. 1:6).

Salvation is a done proposition. Man's responsibility is to accept this by faith, faith alone in Christ alone.

In all the other religions of the world, salvation is a work that man does for God. This is what makes biblical Christianity distinct from all the religions of the world because in the Bible, salvation is of the Lord (Jonah 2:0); it is the work of God for man and Christ's final shout of victory affirmed this truth.

The Necessity of Salvation—The Barrier

In Ephesians 2:14-16 Paul speaks of the barrier of separation which exists between God and man. As long as this barrier exists, there is no possibility of fellowship between God and man. These barriers are;

- Barrier 1: The Holiness of God (Isaiah 57:15) (Hab. 1:13).
- Barrier 2: The Sin of Man (Isaiah 59:1-2) (Romans 3:23)
- Barrier 3: The Penalty of Sin (Romans 3:19-20)
- Barrier 4: Spiritual Death (1 Cor. 15:22) (Romans 6:23)
- Barrier 5: Unrighteousness (Psalm 14:1-3) (Isa. 64:6)

The Removal of the Barrier

Reconciliation is one of the key words of Scripture because it means the sinner, separated and alienated from God by the barrier, can be restored to fellowship with a holy God. How? Through that which God has done for man in His Son, Jesus Christ. This work of God in Christ results in the reconciliation of the believing sinner to God.

The English word "reconcile" means to cause to be friendly again; to bring back to harmony, make peace.

In short, reconciliation is the whole work of

God in Christ by which man is brought from the place of enmity to harmony or peace with God (Rom. 5:1). There are other terms used in Scripture of God's gracious work in Christ like redemption, justification, regeneration, and propitiation, but reconciliation seems to be the over-all term of Scripture which encompasses all the other terms as a part of what God has done through the Lord Jesus to completely remove the enmity or alienation, the whole of the barrier (sin, God's holiness, death, unrighteousness, etc.). It is this work that sets God free to justify the believing sinner by faith in Christ so there is peace with God, the change of relationship from hostility to harmony.

2 Cor 5:18-21 *"And all things are of God, who hath reconciled us to himself by Jesus Christ, and hath given to us the ministry of reconciliation; To wit, that God was in Christ, reconciling the world unto himself, not imputing their trespasses unto them; and hath committed unto us the word of reconciliation. Now then we are ambassadors for Christ, as though God did beseech you by us: we pray you in Christ's stead, be ye reconciled to God. For he hath made him to be sin for us, who knew no*

sin; that we might be made the righteousness of God in him".

From the above scripture, we see that;

- The source of reconciliation is God and not man.

- The agent of reconciliation is the Lord Jesus alone. It is He who personally died for all the world and bore our sin, the cause of alienation, in His body on the tree (Rom. 5:10-11; 2 Cor. 5:18; Col. 1:20-21; 1 Pet. 2:24).

- The object of reconciliation is man.

- The instrument and cause of reconciliation is the death of Jesus Christ on the cross. (2 Cor. 5:21).

- The results of reconciliation;
    - Removal of the barrier (Eph. 2:14-18).

    - Positional sanctification and a perfect standing before God (Rom.

> 5:1; 1 Cor. 1:2; 2 Cor. 5:17; Col. 2:10).
> - Justification (declared righteous before God) through Christ's righteousness imputed to us (2 Cor. 5:18-21).

- The ministers of reconciliation are all believers in Christ. Every believer is an ambassador of Christ and a minister of reconciliation.

Assessments

- Explain the meaning of the word repentance as pertaining to getting saved.

- Explain the terms justification, sanctification and glorification as they relate to salvation.

- As a pastor, describe and explain the process of Salvation to your congregation using Romans chapter 10. Submit your write up to your trainer.

Chapter 7

Bibliology

The term Bibliology (from Greek biblos meaning "book") refers to the study of the nature of the Bible as revelation. It often includes such topics as revelation, inspiration, inerrancy, canonicity, illumination, and interpretation.

The first words of the Bible show that God is the leading character of this divine autobiography: *"In the beginning God . . ."* Its pages show us God taking the initiative, giving us information about Himself and showing his purposes for us—his creation.

Revelation from God

We use the term "revelation" to translate the Greek term "apokalupsis", which means to "unveil" or "uncover." Biblically speaking, revelation is the act and process whereby God makes Himself known to men. This he has done through miracles, visions, dreams, providential control of history, conscience, Jesus Christ, and

Scripture.

Theologians have spoken of **general revelation** through nature (i.e., the created order), conscience, and providentially orchestrated history and **special or particular revelation** primarily in Christ and Scripture (Ps 19:1-6; Rom 1:18-20; 2:14-16; Acts 17:24-34; John 1:14-18).

Jesus Christ was God's fullest and clearest revelation. He is the central theme of the Bible from beginning to end. He who in Genesis is promised as the seed of the woman, is seen in Revelation sitting on the great white throne judging all the races of men.

The Inspiration of the Scriptures

The Bible originated in God's mind, not in human minds. It was given to us by inspiration.

The bible is spoken as "inspired" as mentioned in 2 Timothy 3:16. The word "inspired" is from the Greek word "theopneustos", which literally means "God breathed." To say the Bible is inspired by God means that its origin traces to

God, who is responsible for the words of Scripture (1 Cor 2:13). In 2 Peter 1:21, we find out that the Holy Spirit moved the writers, of the Bible, so that while writing according to their own styles and personalities, the result was God's Word written in authoritative, trustworthy, and free from error in its original autographs. The "autographs" were the original documents that the inspired writer actually wrote upon (not copies or translations).

Inspiration, however, is not limited to mechanical dictation (indeed, very little of it can be said to be mechanical in any way), as we might have, say, in the receiving of the Ten Commandments (or the letters to the churches in Revelation 2-3), but rather occurred in a variety of situations involving the writers as whole people (their minds, emotions, wills, etc.) in their own particular life situations. The end product, however, was always the exact truth God wanted conveyed and carries God's "full weight and authority."

Three terms help us understand the truth of inspiration.

- Plenary inspiration means all of Scripture is inspired—not merely some parts. (Plenary means "full.")

- Verbal inspiration indicates that inspiration extends to the words of the Bible themselves, not only to the ideas.

- Plenary, verbal inspiration stresses the authenticity and reliability of the very words that were written, without depriving the writers of their individuality.

Inerrancy

Since the Bible is inspired by God, it is infallible meaning, "incapable of making mistakes or being wrong." (Matthew 5:18) (John 10:35)

Since God cannot err or deceive, His Word cannot err or deceive and since God is the Supreme Authority in all creation, His Word carries that authority within it to transform lives as stated in Luke 4:31-32 and Hebrews 4:12.

Ancient Writing Materials

Biblical manuscripts, with a few minor exceptions such as verses written on amulets and pots, are written on one of three materials:

- Papyrus - A material similar to thick paper, made from the pith of the papyrus plant that grew along the Nile River in Egypt, very common and cheaper, but wore out more quickly.

- Parchment - Treated animal skins, most durable, but expensive.

- Paper - Early paper was made from rags, e.g. of linen, rather than wood pulp, and it became popular as a writing material only around the twelfth century and was by no means as cheap in the late manuscript era as today.

The books of the Bible

The bible is a book composed of 66 books which are divided into two sections known as Old Testament books and New Testament books.

- The Old Testament contains 39 books;
  - The Pentateuch (Genesis to Deuteronomy) 5 books
  - The History Books (Joshua to Esther) 12 books
  - The Poetry Books (Job to Song of Solomon) 5 books
  - The major prophets (Isaiah to Daniel) 5 books
  - The minor prophets (Hosea to Malachi) 12 books

- The New Testament contains 27 books;
  - The Biographical Books (Matthew to John) 4 books
  - The Historical Book (Acts) 1 book
  - The Doctrinal Books (Romans to Jude) 21 books
  - The prophetical Book (Revelation) 1 book

Canonicity

The Bible, as we know it today, is called the **"canon" of Scripture**, that is, those books recognized as inspired.

- In Jesus' time the Old Testament was viewed as a completed collection. He and the apostles referred to this collection as "the Scripture." Also most of the books of the Old Testament are quoted in the New and always as authoritative.

- The canon of the New Testament, as we know it today, became fixed when Athanasius (A.D. 297-373), considered the father of orthodoxy, listed the books of the New Testament in his thirty-ninth Paschal Letter (A.D. 367). Our canon today was also confirmed at a church council held in Carthage in A.D. 397.

  Three criteria were used in recognizing canonicity:
  - Was a book apostolic in origin?
  - Was the book used and recognized by the churches?
  - Did the book teach sound doctrine?

Based on answers to these three questions, the

orthodox Protestant church today does not receive as canonical the twelve books of the Apocrypha. Also, the Jews never recognized these books as part of their Old Testament.

Illumination

Scripture becomes meaningful to individuals when their hearts are open and illumined by the Holy Spirit. Jesus asked Peter the climactic question, "Who do you say I am?" and Peter's immediate response was, "You are the Christ, the Son of the living God." Jesus then said, "Blessed are you, Simon son of Jonah, for this was not revealed to you by man, but by my Father in heaven" (Matthew 16:15-17, italics added).

Illumination refers to the work of the Spirit in the believer/believing community enabling him/her/them to understand, welcome, and apply inscripturated truth.

Interpretation

Biblical understanding and interpretation can be oversimplified as either "literal" or "figurative."

As when reading anything, including the daily newspaper, some parts of the Bible are to be taken literally and other parts figuratively.

- The Bible uses literary forms such as poetry, allegory, narrative and parable. Though some passages are more perplexing than others, usually common sense helps understanding.

- Figures of speech can be recognized by considering the intent of the author. The Bible is replete with metaphors such as "I am the door" and "I am the vine, you are the branches." Obviously these sentences are not talking about a literal door or wood or tree branches.

- The context of a chapter or book is an excellent starting point for understanding a biblical passage. Statements lifted out of their context can become entirely distorted, even developing into unbiblical doctrines.

- In scripture application, ask yourself these questions;

- Who is the writer or speaker; who is addressed? What is the relationship between the two? What is the primary teaching of the passage? Is there application for us?

- The importance of this cannot be overemphasized. This is applying God's Word to our own lives, personalizing biblical truth and living by it. Application can be universal, applied to all people everywhere; or limited, applied to specific situations, present or future.

Assessment:

1. Why do we all need the Bible, especially in today's society?

2. Why was the Bible written?

Chapter 8

Ecclesiology

Ecclesiology comes from the Greek words ecclesia (church/assembly) and logy (study of). Ecclesiology is the study of the church, its origin, its nature, constitution, ordinances and activities.

The Definitions of the Church

The believers met regularly and *"joined together constantly in prayer"* from the beginning. Acts 1 records 120 of them meeting together. Acts 2 mentions that three thousand were added to the group, and Acts 4 puts the number of believers at five thousand (Acts 1:14-15; 2:41; 4:4). This practice of joining together was what Jesus had called "the church."

The New Testament used the Greek word ekklesia approximately 114 times, which is translated as "church," refers to a "called out" group or "assembly," a word used regularly for secular gatherings of any kind. The Ephesus town clerk, trying to quell a near-riot, said, *"If there is any-thing further you want to bring up, it must be settled in a legal assembly [ekklesia]"* (Acts 19:39).

Applied to Christians, ekklesia meant the church—*"those who have been called out to Jesus Christ."* According to D. W. B. Robinson, it *"mostly means a local congregation of Christians and never a building."*

The definition of a "church" as a separate building specifically for worship was foreign to the early believers, as they met in homes. When a building was mentioned in the New Testament, it was always in relation to the church that met there (Rom 16:5; 1 Cor 16:19; Col 4:15; Philemon 1:2). The church was the people, not the building.

- There are three usages:
    - Of the local assembly of called out ones, "The church in thy house," Philippians 2, The church in the house of Aquila and Priscilla; Romans 16:5, etc

- Of the churches in a province, "Churches in Asia," I Corinthians l6:1; "Churches of the Gentiles," Romans 16:4; "Churches of Macedonia," II Corinthians 8:1; of Judea, Galatians 1:22.

- Of the whole body of Christ, "Christ loved the church," Ephesians 5:25; "Christ is Head of the Church," Ephesians 5:23.

The Origin of the Church

Jesus said in Matthew 16:18 that He will build His church and the gate of hell will not prevail against it. The Church emergences with Jesus Christ and his disciples and was established by the arrival of the Holy Spirit on the day of Pentecost. On that day, Apostle Peter's stood up and preached and *"those who accepted his message were baptized, and about three thousand were added to their number that day"* (Acts 2:41). At first it consisted mainly of Jews who recognized Jesus as the Messiah. Many of them were Hellenists— that is, Greek-speaking

Jews—who had been scattered all over the empire, yet many Jews regularly came to Jerusalem as pilgrims.

The church was then considered a sect within Judaism. One of Paul's accusers referred to him as *"a troublemaker, stirring up riots among the Jews all over the world. He is a ringleader of the Nazarene sect"* (Acts 24:5).

Later, Jewish proselytes (Gentiles who had embraced Judaism) believed the gospel and came into the church. Philip preached the good news in Samaria and later baptized an Ethiopian to whom he had witnessed (Acts 8). Then by a trance the Lord pave the way for gentile Cornelius and his family to be part of the church through reluctant Peter (Acts 10:9-16).

Other Christian Jews preached the gospel in Antioch, where a mixed church of Jews and Gentiles came into existence (Acts 13:1). It was here in Antioch that believers were first called Christians or "Christ's men" (Acts 11:26).

The Purposes of the Church

The New Testament mentions many roles of the church, below are;

- Serves as Christ Kingdom executives that exist to excuse the will of the Lord on the earth (Matt 6:10)
- Present the gospel of Jesus (Mark 16:15)
- Teach doctrine (Matthew 28:20)
- Guide believers in righteousness and good works (2 Timothy 3:15-17)
- Building each other up in Christ (Ephesians 2:19-22)
- Confront sin (Matthew 18:15-20)
- Mutual accountability (Acts 20:28)
- Developing and serving with spiritual gifts (1 Corinthians 12)
- Providing each other support in trials and rejoicing in good times (1 Cor 12:25-26)
- Maturing believers in faith (Jude 1:20)
- Perfecting believers for ministry (Eph 4:11-13)
- Giving guidance against false doctrine (Ephesians 4:11-15)

Church Government

Christ is Head of the Church. (I Cor 11:3) (Eph 1:22, 5:23) (Col 1:18)

Also throughout the history of the church, there have been several different, yet basic forms of church government. These include:

- In the **Episcopalian** form of government, the archbishop has authority over the bishop, who in turn presides over a diocese, i.e., several churches, which is cared for by the rector or vicar. The archbishop, bishop, and rectors are all ordained priests within the Episcopal system of church government. This form of government can be seen in the Methodist, Anglican, and in its most hierarchical form the Catholic Church. This system is actually not found in the New Testament. Those who hold to this type of church government, however, feel that it was a natural development in the second-century church.

- **Presbyterian** form of church governance

typified by the rule of assemblies of presbyters, or elders. Each local church is governed by a body of elected elders usually called the session or church board. Groups of local churches are governed by a higher assembly of elders known as the presbytery or classis; presbyteries can be grouped into a synod, and presbyteries and synods nationwide often join together in a general assembly. Responsibility for conduct of church services is reserved to an ordained minister or pastor known as a teaching elder, or a minister of the word and sacrament. Presbyterian polity was developed as a rejection of governance by hierarchies of single bishops (episcopal polity), but also differs from the congregationalist polity. Only the presbytery can ordain ministers, install pastors, and start up, close, and approve relocating a congregation and the moderator and officers are elected by and from among the members of the assembly.

- The local congregation is autonomous in

the **congregational** form of church government. His is also known as one man church governments. E.g: Baptists, the Evangelical Free Church, the Open Brethren, Christians (Disciples), and some Bible and other independent churches. Followers of this polity hold that no one person or group should exercise authority over a local congregation of Christ's church. With some exceptions, these churches have two types of ministers—pastors and deacons.

Church Ordinances

There are numerous differences of opinion about the number and nature of ordinances or sacraments in the church. Ordinances are outward rites that signify or represent spiritual grace or blessing. The Roman Catholic Church has seven sacraments: baptism, the Lord's Supper, confirmation, penance, orders, matrimony and extreme unction.

The protestants maintain, however, that Scripture recognizes only two ordinances—

baptism and the Lord's Supper.

Gifts given to the Church
- 5fold Ministry (Eph 4:11-12)
- Body Ministries (Romans 12:4-8)
- Spiritual gifts (1 Cor 12:1,7-11)

Assessment:
- Should Church service be held on Saturday or Sunday? Discuss

- Differentiate between a local church and a ministry.

Chapter 9

Eschatology

The term "eschatology" comes from two Greek terms escato" and lovgo" meaning "last, end, or final" and "study of," respectively. Theologically speaking, then, the term eschatology refers to "the study of final things or The Last Days" in the Bible.

To rightly divide the Word is to know the times in which they were spoken, and again the time to which they refer. Any text should tell:

- Time which written
- People to whom written
- Lesson derived from it

Dispensations

Ephesians 1:10 *"That in the dispensation of the fullness of times he might gather together in one all things in Christ, both which are in heaven, and which are on earth; even in him"*

A dispensation is a period of time during which man is tested in respect of obedience to some specific revelation of the will of God." C. I. Scofield, Reference Bible, note 4, page 5.

Dispensationalism has this wonderful fact very plainly in the forefront. "God has dealt in the different dispensations with different methods." Understanding this truth will make your understanding of the last days easier because one of the greatest advances in the understanding of the whole Bible and its complete message is to know the various dispensations. This helps in the Scriptural injunction, "Rightly dividing the Word of Truth," II Timothy 2:15.

Looking through the Bible, we can find seven distinct dispensations that were God-ordered and God-ordained. Each dispensation has a purpose in the overall story. The following is a brief description of each dispensation.

The Seven Dispensations

1. The Dispensation of Innocence: This dispensation covers the time from the creation of man to the fall of man (Genesis 1:28-30 and 2:15-17). All of

God's creatures lived at peace with themselves and with each other, and the world was without sin or death. Man was to procreate, rule the earth and the animals, and take care of the garden. He was given one command to obey: not to eat of the tree of the knowledge of good and evil. Eve and Adam disobeyed this rule, and were expelled from the garden as punishment, ending the dispensation of innocence.

2. The Dispensation of Conscience: The expulsion from the garden began the dispensation of conscience—a time when man was left to rule himself by his own will and conscience, both of which had been tainted by sin. It was a disaster, and ended in disaster—the worldwide flood (Genesis 3:8—8:22). During this dispensation, man became so wicked that "every intention of the thoughts of his heart was only evil continually" and God regretted making man and was "grieved to his heart" (Genesis 6:5-6). This was also the time when fallen angels married human women and produced giant, evil

offspring called Nephilim (Genesis 6:1-4). God chose to end humanity with a flood and begin again with Noah and his family (Genesis 6:11-18).

3. The Dispensation of Human Government: The dispensation of human government began just after the flood. God made promises and gave commands to Noah and his family. God promised not to curse the earth again, and never to flood it again. He commanded Noah and his sons to repopulate the world and scatter across the earth, and He allowed them to use animals for food. God also established the law of capital punishment (Genesis 8:1-9:7). Noah's descendants failed to "fill the earth" as was commanded, and instead they worked together to build the tower of Babel (Genesis 11:1-9). God countered this action by confusing their languages, creating different nations and cultures that later spread to different areas. This was the beginning of human government.

4. The Dispensation of Promise: The

dispensation of human government lasted until the call of Abraham. The call of Abraham, the lives of the patriarchs, and the enslavement of the Jewish people to Egypt all fall under the dispensation of promise. This was the time when Abraham's descendants waited for the promise that was given to Abraham: that God would make Abraham's descendants a great nation and give them their own land (Genesis 12:1-7). This dispensation ended with the Exodus of the Jews from Egypt. Once they left Egypt they were officially a nation, led by God into the wilderness toward the Promised Land.

5. The Dispensation of Law: The dispensation of law lasted almost 1,500 years, beginning with the Exodus and ending with the crucifixion and resurrection of Jesus Christ. The delivery of the Ten Commandments and the Mosaic Law, found in Exodus 19—23, outlined the standard of perfection that God required from His people, and included the instructions about temple worship and sacrifices. This was the age

of priests, prophets and kings, both good and evil. The people of Yahweh repeatedly broke His commands, and wandered off after other gods. It is important to note that strict following of commandments was never as important to God as mercy and faithfulness (Hosea 6:6). The law was given to show the people that they needed to depend on God and trust Him to save them, rather than trusting themselves, their own goodness, or other gods for salvation. He has never expected perfection—if He did, He would not have provided the sacrificial system as a way for man to say "yes, I have sinned; here is a symbol of my need for forgiveness and atonement." The blood of bulls and goats cannot take away sin—they are a symbol, looking forward to the One whose blood could take away sin (Hebrews 9:11-14; Hebrews 10:3-10).

6. The Dispensation of Grace: This dispensation started at the resurrection of Jesus Christ and continues today. It is the new covenant in Christ's blood (Luke

22:20). This is also called the "age of grace" or the "church age," and scholars believe that the entire dispensation— more than 2,000 years—occurs between the 69th and 70th weeks of Daniel's prophecy in Daniel 9:24. Atonement was provided on the cross, once for all, for any who would believe: Abraham's children are all those who have faith, including Gentiles (or non-Jews) (Hebrews 10:10, 14; Romans 5:1; Romans 3:29-30; Galatians 3:7, 29). During this dispensation, we also have a Comforter with us, the Holy Spirit of God, who indwells believers (John 14:16-26). Dispensationalists believe that the Church Age will end with the rapture of the Church (1 Thessalonians 4:13-18; Revelation 3:10) and then the tribulation, the seven years when those who dwell on the earth will experience God's judgment, will begin (Daniel 12:1-4; Matthew 24:21-27).

7. The Dispensation of the Millennial Kingdom of Christ: This dispensation will last for 1,000 years as Christ

Himself rules on earth. This Kingdom will fulfill the prophecy to the Jewish nation that Christ will return and be their King. The only people allowed to enter the Kingdom are the born-again believers from the Age of Grace, righteous survivors of the seven years of tribulation, and the resurrected Old Testament saints. No unsaved person is allowed access into this kingdom. Satan is bound during the 1,000 years. This period ends with the final judgment (Revelation 20:11-14). The old world is destroyed by fire, and the New Heaven and New Earth of Revelation 21 and 22 will begin.

The Final Generation

Matthew 24:34 *"Verily I say unto you, this generation shall not pass, till all these things be fulfilled. Heaven and earth shall pass away, but my words shall not pass away".*

The Last Generation Prophesied (Pro 30:11-14)

The Last Generation Church Described (Revelation 3:14-22).

The Last Generation Exposed (2 Timothy 3:1-8, 13). Let us analyze these verses:

- **Verse 1** – *"This know also that in the last days perilous times shall come."*
  - The Bible makes it unmistakably plain that in the last days, the world will be filled with difficulties, the like of which have never before been known in the history of mankind.

  - Perilous times carries the connotation of evil morality, harsh nations and dangerous people. In such times, you shall see wars, deadly diseases and plagues, violence, crime, suicide, terrorists, disasters, etc.

- **Verse 2** – *"For men shall be lovers of their own selves."*

- The god of self: me, myself and I. This is also known as the religion of humanism.

- Covetous: Those who desperately try to keep up with the Joneses, loving the world and the things of this world.

- Boasters: Those who can't say enough about themselves.

- Proud: People who take personal credit for what God enables them to do.

- Blasphemers: Those who mock God or Jesus and use His name in vain.

- Disobedient to parents: Children in rebellion to their parents' authority.

- Unthankful: They don't show appreciation to God and to thos who helped them.

- Unholy: People who are sinful and practice unrighteousness.

- **Verse 3** – *"Without natural affection."*

  - Does not care about babies hence promote abortion

  - Some show more affection shown towards dogs and cats today than towards wives, husbands, children, neighbors, or friends.

  - Truce breakers: Breaking promises. Peace treaties have become an exercise in futility.

  - False Accusers: A false accusation is a claim or allegation of wrongdoing that is untrue and/or otherwise unsupported by facts. There are people who can lie and accuse people falsely.

  - Incontinent: This means a lack of self-restraint or chastity; seeking instant gratification for every lust of the flesh or eyes.

- Fierce: Violence in sports, movies, TV, between countries, factions, sects, etc.

- Despisers of those that are good: Any president our country has doesn't stand a chance against the vicious pens of those who hate capitalism. Godly men and women are condemned today as evildoers living on the lunatic fringe.

- **Verse 4** – *"Traitors."*
    - This means to make a decision rashly; being headstrong.

    - High minded: Thinking of yourself to be better than you are.

    - Lovers of pleasure more than lovers of God: Sundays have become a day of recreation, rather than a day of church attendance and service.

- **Verse 5** – *"Having a form of godliness, but denying the power thereof: from such turn away."*

  - Attend Church but visit the shrine for assistance.

  - Teaching the word of God but does not believe in miracles.

  - Believing the cessation of the gifts of the Holy Spirit.

  - Attends church but does not believe in the save by grace through faith without works.

- **Verse 6** – *"Silly women laden with sins, led away with divers lusts."*

  - Being a slave to lust and incapable of controlling themselves or saving themselves for their husbands.

- Projecting sexuality through TV, billboards, movies, in music, magazines, social media, etc.

- **Verse 7** – *"Ever learning and never able to come to the knowledge of the truth."*
  - Rejecting the simple truth but accumulating more knowledge and operating with common sense.

- **Verse 8** – *"Resist the truth."*
  - Jesus is the truth (John 14:6). God has said that His Word is the truth. When the true Word of God is preached today, there is a resistance to our yielding to that truth.

  - Men of corrupt minds: The imagination of men's hearts is only evil continually. Who would have ever thought the Constitution would be used to protect pornographers and throw the Bible out of the schools?

- Reprobate concerning the faith: A reprobate is a scoundrel. Certainly religion has been rocked by scoundrels lately who appeared for a while as Christian ministers.

- **Verse 13** – *"But evil men and seducers shall wax worse and worse, deceiving and being deceived."*

  - Evil will rise and deception will be rampant.

This signs are all seen in this generation, indicating to us that we are in the final generation.

The signs of the end-times can be group into;
- Moral Sign
- Jewish Sign
- Gentile Nation's Sign
- Social Sign
- Church Sign

The rapture of the Church

The word "rapture" does not appear in the Bible

so as the word "Trinity," or "Missionary" nevertheless are biblical and describes the truth of God's word.

The word "rapture" refers to a Latin term that means to be "caught up." The Bible speaks clearly of a time when believers in Jesus will be taken to be with Him in an instant. This event can take place at any moment

- Specifics of The Rapture
    - Biblical Synonyms:
        - ✓ Translated (Hebrews 11:5)
        - ✓ Caught up (2 Corinthians 12:2,4).
        - ✓ Resurrection (Romans 6:5).
        - ✓ Notice also the word "rise" in 1 Thessalonians 4:16.

    - Characteristics of the Rapture
        - ✓ Christ Himself will come to the clouds (Acts 1:11)
        - ✓ The Lord will shout (1 Thes 4:16) (Rev 4:1)
        - ✓ The voice of the archangel will be heard (1 Thes 4:16)

- ✓ Sounding of the trumpet (1 Cor 15:52) (1 Thes4:16)
- ✓ The dead in Christ shall rise first (1 Thes 4:16)
- ✓ Then those alive in Christ shall be caught up (1 Thes 4:17) (1 Cor 15:52).
- ✓ The saved will meet the Lord in the clouds (1 Thes 4:17).
- ✓ In this moment we shall all be changed (1 Cor 15:51-54).
- ✓ Our transformation will be in a twinkling of an eye (1 Cor 15:52).
- ✓ All the saved will be with the Lord forever (1 Thes 4:17).

- ▪ Examples of Raptures
  - ✓ Enoch - (Genesis 5:24). Also read Hebrews 11:5.
  - ✓ Elijah - (2 Kings 2:11).
  - ✓ Jesus Christ - (Acts 1:9).
  - ✓ The Two Witnesses - (Revelation 11:3,12).

The Christian's Judgment In Heaven (the "Judgment Seat of Christ") (Romans 14:10). (2 Corinthians 5:10).

"Judgment Seat" is from the Greek word "BEMA" which means "a foot-breath, rostrum or tribunal." It is sometimes a reference to the judgment box that a referee stood in high above the Greek Olympic stadiums (like a press box). There he would watch to see who won and who ran according to the rules. Those who won races climbed to the top of the steps in the stadium to have an olive-leaf crown placed on their heads (a corruptible crown - 1 Corinthians 9:25). Let's look at the facts of this day:

- Every single Christian shall stand before the judgment seat of Christ (Romans 14:10).

- Every tongue shall make confession to God (Romans 14:11).

- Every knee shall bow to the Lord Jesus Christ. The same is said of the unsaved – (Philippians 2:10).

- Everyone shall give an account of himself to God (Rom 14:12) (1 Cor 3:13-15). The word "account" comes from the Greek word "logos," and literally means "a log, computation." This accounting will not be of our sins (Romans 4:8), but of our works for God after salvation. (2 Cor 5:10). Good – as living sacrifices. Read Romans 12:1; Galatians 5:24-25. Bad– living for ourselves. Read Romans 8:13.

- Everything we have done with ourselves since salvation will be tested by fire (1 Cor 3:13).

- Whatever was done for God and with God's help will be rewarded (1 Cor 3:14). These rewards may be:

  - Royal Rewards (Crowns)
    - ✓ Crown of Life (for a life of self-crucifixion) whether physical martyrdom (Rev 2:10) or spiritual martyrdom (James 1:12).

- ✓ Incorruptible Crown - A reward for running by the rules (1Cor 9:24-27).

- ✓ Crown of Righteousness - Those who live as though Christ could come any moment (2 Tim 4:8).

- ✓ Crown of Glory- An elder's crown for setting good example (1 Peter 5:4).

- ✓ Crown of Rejoicing - A crown just for soul-winners (1 Thes. 2:19).

- ▪ Other rewards
  - ✓ Prophets Reward (Matthew 10:41)
  - ✓ For faithfulness (Matt 25:21-23)
  - ✓ For positions (Col 3:18-24; 4:1) For being a good wife, husband, child, father, employee, or employer

- ✓ For willingness (1 Cor 9:17)
- ✓ For giving (Phil 4:15-18; Rom 15:28; Matt 6:19-20) God is a meticulous record keeper
- ✓ For fellowship, fearing God & thinking upon God (Malachi 3:16-17)
- ✓ For loving others (Matthew 5:44-48)
- ✓ For being persecuted (Matthew 5:12; Luke 6:22-23)

- Whatever was done for self and in the flesh will be burned up and lost forever (1 Cor 3:15; 2 John 1:8)

- Every Christian shall receive some reward, whether great or little (Rev 22:12; 1 Cor 3:8; Eph 6:8)

The Marriage Supper of the Lamb

This will take place in heaven, just prior to Jesus riding back to earth. (Rev 19:1-8). It will probably happen towards the end of the 7-year tribulation on earth and probably after the Judgment Seat of Christ. It should be noted here that there are no physical marriages of husbands and wives in Heaven (see Luke 20:27-40).

- God's People are Referred to as His Spiritual Wife
    - Israel (Isaiah 54:5) (Jeremiah 3:14)

    - The New Testament Church
        - Christ portrayed as the Bridegroom (Matthew 9:15).

        - The church portrayed as His bride or wife (Romans 7:4).

        - The church today is espoused to Christ (2 Cor 11:2)

            - To "espouse" means "to marry, take up, or make one's own. (Matthew 1:18-25).

Likewise, we are legally married to Christ though currently separated from Him physically. This is a time of proving by self-discipline and commitment.

- At the Rapture, the Church is Taken to the Marriage Supper of the Lamb as portrayed in the parable of the 10 virgins (Matthew 25:1-13) and the parable of the marriage of the king's son (Matthew 22:1-14).

- The Lord Himself will Serve the Dinner After the Wedding (Luke 12:37).

The Seven-Year Tribulation on Earth

While Christians are in Heaven being judged and experiencing the Marriage Supper of the Lamb, those left on earth will be experiencing tribulation such as the world has never seen (Matthew 24:21)

- The Tribulation Defined
    - A Time of Jacob's (Israel's) Trouble (Jeremiah 30:7).

    - The Great Tribulation (Rev 7:14). (Deut 4:30-31)

    - Daniel's' 70th week (Daniel 9:24-27). A week is 7 years (Gen 29:27).

- The Events Of The Tribulation (In Probable Order)
    - Immediate War: A war will break out between various Eastern Bloc and Middle East countries against Israel. Read Ezekiel 38 and 39. God delivers Israel miraculously.

    - The Anti-Christ's Rise: The Anti-Christ will sign a 7-year covenant of peace with Israel (Daniel 8:25; 1 Thes 5:3). He will break that covenant in the midst of "the week" (after 3½ years) and shall sit in the temple, controlling the world and declaring that he is God. This event

113

is called the "abomination of desolation" in Matthew 24:15; Mark 13:14. The Anti-Christ is described in further detail in 2 Thessalonians 2:3-10; Daniel 8:23-25.

- Temple in Jerusalem Rebuilt: This is told in Ezekiel 40-48. Note the existence of the temple at the midway point of the tribulation in (2 Thes 2:4)

- God's Two Witnesses Begin to Preach: "And I will give power unto my two witnesses, and they shall prophesy a thousand two hundred and threescore days, clothed in sackcloth." (Revelation11:3).

- Book with Seven Seals is Opened: Each seal reveals something that will happen on earth. This is told in Revelation5.
  - First seal (Revelation 6:2). The anti-Christ begins to rule.

➢ Second seal (Revelation 6:3,4). Peace is taken from the earth and replaced by a great sword (possibly a reference to the previously mentioned war in Ezekiel 38-39).

➢ Third seal (Revelation 6:5-6). A world-wide famine.

➢ Fourth seal (Rev 6:7,8). One-quarter of those living on earth are killed.

➢ Fifth seal (Rev 6:9-11). The martyrdom of believers on earth.

➢ Sixth seal (Rev 6:12-17). A great earthquake.

➢ God's mark and seal on His own (Rev 14:1-5). Following the opening of the Sixth seal, God marks his children on their foreheads and seals 144,000 who will be witnesses for Him. These 144,000 are Jews.

- ➢ Seventh seal: This part of the sealed book reveals seven angels, sounding seven trumpets of Judgment. This is all told in Revelation 8:1 - 11:19.
    - ✓ First trumpet (Rev 8:7) one-third of trees and grass are burnt up.
    - ✓ Second trumpet (Rev 8:8-9) one-third of the sea becomes blood, one-third of all water life dies, one-third of all ships destroyed.
    - ✓ Third trumpet (Rev 8:10-11) one-third of the earth's water becomes bitter.
    - ✓ Fourth trumpet (Rev 8:12) one-third part of daylight removed.
    - ✓ Fifth trumpet (Rev 9:1-12) hideous satanic demons torment unbelievers on earth for 5 months.

- ✓ Sixth trumpet (Rev 9:13) one-third of all men killed in war.
- ✓ Two witnesses are slain (Rev 11:7-12) the witnesses from God, who tormented unbelievers with their preaching, are slain and left dead in the streets for 3½ days. They resurrect and ascend into Heaven.
- ✓ The seventh trumpet sounds (Rev 11:15) lightning, voices, thunder, earthquake and great hail.

- ➤ The Beast and False Prophet Rise; The Beast is the one-world political leader. The False Prophet is the one-world religious leader. These will rise to full prominence and control the entire world. Read Rev 13.

- ➤ The Gospel is Preached to All the World (Rev 14:6).

> ➢ The Seven Vial Judgments On the Earth (Rev 16:1).
>   - ✓ First vial - (Rev 16:2).
>   - ✓ Second vial - (Rev 16:3).
>   - ✓ Third vial - (Rev 16:4).
>   - ✓ Fourth vial - (Rev 16:8-9).
>   - ✓ Fifth vial - (Rev 16:10-11).
>   - ✓ Sixth vial - (Rev 16:12-16).
>   - ✓ Seventh vial - (Rev 16:17-21).

The Battle of Armageddon

The preparation for the battle (The Sixth Vial)

- The river euphrates is dried up (Rev 16:12). The Euphrates river is called "the great river." It starts in Armenia (Turkey) and runs through Iraq, Babylon and into the Persian Gulf. It is one of the great rivers of the world.

- The way is prepared for the kings of the East (Rev 16:12). These "kings of the east" are probably the Russian States, Iran,

Turkey, Iraq, Red China, etc. They will be prepared for conventional warfare.

- Unclean Spirits (Devils) Come from the World's Leaders (Rev 16:13). The devils come out of the mouth of the Dragon (the Devil - Revelation 20:2), the Beast (the world's political ruler), and the False Prophet (the one-world religious leader). This may mean that the demons inhabit the words and instruction that this unholy trinity gives.

- These Devils Gather an Army (Rev 16:14). Using man's gullibility, the devils do miracles, go into every nation of the world and begin gathering the largest army in history – from every nation in the whole world.

- God's Mercy is Still Extended (Rev 16:15). Despite God's wrath being poured out on the world, His mercy is still extended, and the saved on earth are encouraged to watch and be ready. (Matt 25:13) and (1 Thes 5:5-10).

- The Nations are Gathered Together into a Place Called Armageddon (Rev 16:16). Armageddon means "the mountain of Megiddo." Megiddo means "the place of troops." This is a historical battlefield:

  - Sisera - The captain of the host of Canaan was defeated by Barak and Deborah by the Waters of Megiddo (Judges 5:19-20).

  - Ahaziah - The king of Judah died at Megiddo after being pursued by the zealous Jehu (2 Kings 9:27).

  - Josiah - The righteous king of Judah was killed while fighting against the army of Pharoah-necho (2 Kings 23:29).

  - ❖ Note: Between the preparation for the Battle of Armageddon and the battle itself is the destruction of the Great Whore (ecumenical religion) in Rev 17, and the destruction of

Babylon (the world's material system) in Rev 18.

- The Battle Participants
    - The Lord Jesus Christ - With all of His glorious names, Jesus Christ rides on a white horse in power and splendor (Rev. 19:11-13,16,19).

    - The armies of heaven - These follow Jesus on white horses and in fine, white linen (Revelation 19:14,19)

    - The lost nations and armies of this world: This includes the Beast, the kings of the earth, and all their armies. (Revelation 19:15,18-19)

- The Battle
    - The enemies of the Lord are smitten by the power of His Word Rev 19:15 (compare with Hebrews 4:12). Notice the reference to the wine press in Rev 14:19-20.

Sixteen hundred furlongs equals about 200 miles.

- The Beast is captured (Revelation 19:20)

- The false prophet is captured (Rev 19:20)

- They are cast into a Lake of Fire (Rev 19:20)

- All the rest of the armies are slain (Rev 19:21) These are slain by the power of the Lord's Sword, which is His Word.

- The flesh of all these armies is devoured by vultures (Rev 19:17-18,21)

The Judgment of Nations

The Judgment of the nations before the millennium; It is Prophesied that:-

- Christ will Rule the Nations of the World Someday (Isaiah 9:6-7) (Rev 19:15)

- Christ will Share His Reign (Matt 24:46-48). We must be found faithful, wise, and suffering for His sake. See 2 Timothy 3:12. Christ will be the Head, but we will share this reign:

  - We shall reign over the nations with a rod of iron (Rev 2:26-27)

  - We shall reign on the earth (Revelation 5:9-10)

  - We may be placed in authority over cities or a nation (Luke 19:11-19)

  - We shall reign for 1000 years (Revelation 20:4-6)

- The judgment of the nations after the millennium
  - The Nations Shall be Judged (Matt 25:31-32) (Psalms 9:17) (Rom 11:26).

- Individual cities shall be judged (Matt 10:11, 14-15) (Matt 11:21-24). This judgment of cities could take place during the tribulation period. Christians should strive to be the salt of the earth where they live.

The Millennial Kingdom

The Kingdom of Christ on earth (Isaiah 9:6-7). "Millennium" means "one thousand years." It is mentioned six times in the first seven verses of Rev 20. Let us study the details of these thousand years:

- Satan will be bound (Rev 20:1-3). The tempter of the saved and unsaved, the accuser of the brethren, will be bound 1000 years in a bottomless pit. He will not be able to deceive the nations (people) during this time.

- Christians will rule and reign (Rev 20:4). God's promise to let believers rule and reign with Christ will come to pass.

- Believers will be resurrected (Rev 20:6). Those who died in Christ during the tribulation are resurrected to be with and reign with Him.

- Christians will also be priests (Rev 20:6). We will not only rule and reign, but we will also be priests of God and Christ. See also Revelation 1:6, 5:10. A priest is one who makes intercession, a go-between, one who prays for another. Why will we need to be priests during Christ's Kingdom? Because;

- Lost people will still be living on earth (Revelation 20:7-8). Remember, about half of the world's population survives the tribulation and makes it into the millennium. By today's account that would be over 3 billion.

- Man will procreate during the millennium (Isaiah 65:20). What could the world's population explode to in 1,000 years if death were very limited?

- There will be death (Isaiah 65:20). Because there will still be sin and sinners, there will still be death. See Romans 6:23a.

- Life will go on (Isaiah 65:21).

- We will not lose what we worked for (Isaiah 65:22-23). Neither the government nor anyone else will take what we have worked for, for God is a giver, not a taker.

- We will receive an answer before we pray (Isaiah 65:24).

- The nature of animals shall change (Isaiah 65:25). See also Isaiah 11:6-8.

- There will only be peace (Isaiah 66:12a) See also Isaiah 11:9.

- The whole earth shall be full of the knowledge of the Lord (Isaiah 11:9).

- God's people will have rest (Isaiah 11:10).

The Great White Throne Judgment

Resurrection of the wicked dead; Let us look at the facts of this resurrection and judgment:

- This will Take Place Right after:
    - The Millennium Reign of Christ on earth (Revelation 20:1-6)

    - The final overthrow of Satan (Revelation 20:7-10)

    - The final war (Revelation 20:8-9)

- There will be a Great White Throne (Rev 20:11a). The word "great" is a very general word (Greek – "megas") which, appropriately in this text, means large.

- God Himself sits upon this Throne (Rev 20:11-12). The earth and the heaven fled away from the presence of the great God.

- This is a judgment of the "Dead" (Rev 20:12) This refers to those that are dead in their trespasses and sins, not the saved.

- Both small and great shall be there
    - Small (Greek - "mikros") Meaning small in size or dignity. Sometimes translated "little" in the English (for example: Matthew 10:42 and Matthew 18:14 – references to children).

    - Great (Greek - "megas") This is the same word as used in point 2 above, describing the White Throne. Great in dignity or stature (sometimes referring to adults).

- They Will Stand Before God Himself (Rev 20:12)

- The Books Will Be Opened (Rev 20:12) The Bible is the "books" mentioned here (See Daniel 7:10; John 12:48). The word "Bible" means "library." It contains 66 books. God is going to judge man by the Bible. Man is responsible to know God's

Word and is accountable for what it says. Having rejected the finished work of Christ, the dead will be judged according to their works. No man's works are good enough to save his own soul. Read (Isaiah 64:6; Ephe 2:8-9; Titus 3:5)

- Another Book Is Opened – the Book of Life (Revelation 20:12)
  - Those written in the Book are God's people (Daniel 12:1 and Luke 10:20). It is the present condition of the saved to have their names in the Book of Life.

  - Those in the Book have a passport to the New Jerusalem (Rev 21:27) Having one's name written in the Lamb's Book of Life is a passport to enter the New Jerusalem, God's Holy City.

  - To be written in the Book of Life, one must be saved. Compare Revelation3:5 with 1 John 5:4-5. Those who are saved have had their sins cleansed in the Blood of

Jesus Christ (Rev 1:5) and the Lord does not impute sin to their account (Romans 4:7,8).

- Sinners will be blotted out of the Book of Life (Exodus 32:33) tells us that initially the name of every human being is in the Book of Life. But any person who has one sin imputed to them will be blotted out of this Book.

- Those blotted out of the Book of Life are the devil's people (Rev 13:8; 17:8)

- The Resurrection of the Dead (Rev 20:13).
    - The sea gave up the dead. This is a reference to the resurrection of the body.

    - Death and hell delivered up the dead which were in them. This is a reference to the resurrection of the soul. "Death and Hell" are inseparable for the unsaved.

(Psalms 55:15); (Pro 5:5); (Rev 6:8); and (Rev 20:14). These are delivered up to the Great White Throne judgment.

The Second Death

Death and Hell are cast into the Lake of Fire. (Rev 20:14)

- Death:- 1 Corinthians 15:26 tells us that death is the last enemy that shall be destroyed.

- Hell:- Hell has been the "holding center" for the lost, before they are cast into the Lake of Fire.

  - This process is called "the second death." "And death and hell were cast into the lake of fire. This is the second death." (Rev 20:14) The first death is physical but the second is eternal punishment (Rev 2:11; 20:6; 21:8; Jude 1:12) and all unbelievers are cast into the Lake of Fire. (Rev 20:15)

Restoration of the New Heaven and New Earth

- New Heaven
    - Prophesied (Isaiah 65:17; Isaiah 66:22; Matthew 5:18; Matthew 24:35; Mark 13:31; Luke 21:33; Hebrews 12:25-29)

    - Fulfilled (2 Peter 3:10,13; Revelation 21:1)

    - Destruction of Present Heavens
        - Dissolved with fire (Isaiah 34:4; 2 Peter 3:12)

        - Rolled back like a scroll (Isaiah 34:4; Revelation 6:14)

    - Creation of New Heaven (Isaiah 65:17; 66:22) a direct creative act of God

- New Earth
    - Prophesied (Isaiah 65:17; Isaiah 66:22; Matthew 5:18; Matthew 24:35; Mark 13:31; Luke 21:33;

> Hebrews 12:25-29; Revelation 21:5)

- Fulfilled (2 Peter 3:7-14; Revelation 21:1)

- Destruction of present earth
  - Destroyed by fire (2 Peter 3:7)

  - Destroyed by fervent heat (2 Peter 3:10,12)

- Creation of New Earth (Isaiah 65:17; 66:22) a direct creative act of God

Eternity

We have seen the eternity of the dead (those lost in sins) described early of this study (The Great White Throne Judgment). This section refers to the eternity that will be enjoyed by the saved. It can best be described by the word "new."

- The New Heaven (Revelation 21:1).

- A place the Lord is preparing for us now (John 14:2b)
- A place of treasure laid up for us (Matthew 6:20)
- A place where the names of the saved are written (Luke 10:20)
- A place of many mansions (John 14:2)
- A place where the glory of God and Jesus can be seen (Acts 7:55-56)
- A place where all the redeemed live in the presence of god and Christ (Rev 7:9) this will include people from all nations, kindreds, people and tongues

- The New Earth (Rev 21:1)
  - No more sea (Rev 21:1)
  - The place where the new Jerusalem will be transplanted (Rev 21:1)
  - A place where God Himself will be with us (Rev 21:3)
  - A place of no tears, death, sorrow, crying or pain (Rev 21:4)
  - A place that will continue to have nations and Kings (Rev 21:24-26;

22:2) Christians who have earned the right to do so will continue to reign forever (Revelation 2:26; 22:5).

- The New Jerusalem - (Hebrews 13:14) Read also Hebrews 10:9-10; 15-16.

  - Names
    - New Jerusalem (Rev 3:12; 21:2)
    - The Holy City (Rev 21:2)
    - The Holy Jerusalem (Rev 21:10) Note: the present Jerusalem has become very unholy (Rev 11:8)
    - The Tabernacle of God (Rev 21:3)

  - Location (Rev 21:1-2) It will be transplanted from heaven where it is being built (John 14:2b) to the New Earth (Rev 21:9-10). It is compared to twice as a bride prepared for her husband. Everything is perfect.

  - Description (All told in Rev 21)

➢ Lighting (Rev 21:11,23-24; 22:5) The brilliancy of God's Being lights it.

➢ An outer wall (Rev 21:12-13) This wall goes around the city, on the outside.
  ✓ It is four-sided (Revelation 21:13)
  ✓ There are three gates on each side (Rev 21:13) Each gate has a name of one of the tribes of Israel on it. Angels are stationed at the gates at all times.
  ✓ It is approximately 216 feet high (Revelation 21:17) A man's cubit is about 18"
  ✓ It is made of jasper (Revelation 21:18)

➢ The City Wall - The city is encompassed by a wall inside the outer wall. The dimensions of that wall are much greater than those of the outer wall.

- ✓ It's height, length, and width are equal (Revelation 21:16) They are 12,000 furlongs. A furlong is approximately 1/8 mile. Thus, the dimensions are foursquare: 1500 miles wide, 1500 miles long, 1500 miles high.

- ✓ It has 12 foundations (Revelation 21:14) Each one has the name of one of the Apostles of Christ on it. (Do not confuse this with the outer wall!)

- ✓ Each foundation is made of a different type of stone (Revelation 21:19-21)

- ➢ Inside the City - Described in Revelation 21:18-27. What is there?

> ✓ Pure gold and streets of gold (Revelation 21:18,21)
> ✓ The Lord (Revelation 21:22)
> ✓ Pure river of water of life (Revelation 21: 22:1)
> ✓ The tree of life (Revelation 2:7 and 22:2,14)
> ✓ Many mansions (John 14:1)
> ✓ The saved (Revelation 21:24 and 22:3-4)

❖ Note: A comparison of Rev 22:14 and 22:19 seems to indicate that not every Christian is going to have total access to the Holy City. Only those that have earned it in this life. Let us strive to keep His works until the end – not for salvation, but for reward's sake. (See Rev 2:26)

- New Everything - (Revelation 21:5a) Compare Isaiah 65:17.

- New Name - (Isaiah 56:5). See also Isaiah 62:2; Revelation 2:17; 3:12. In the Bible, whenever God gave a new name to something or somebody, it was an accurate description of that thing or person. What may God name you?

- New Song - "And they sung a new song...." (Revelation 5:9a).

Assessment: How different is the judgment of the sheep from that of the goats?

ESSAY: Prepare and present a theological lesson on women in ministry.

Contact Information

I would love to hear from you as a writer, I welcome a personal email from you. One way to really bless me, however, is to write an honest review of any length of this book on Amazon. This helps others decide if they should buy this book. Writing a review costs you nothing, and it is one way to let me know that you enjoyed the book. Please take the time to do so, even if you have never written one before. You can email me and give me feedback, share your story with me or send me a prophetic word at princesinbad3000@gmail.com

To know more about my ministry, have me ministry at your events, support my ministry financially or to request your own personal prophecy, prayer of deliverance or healing, you can visit my website at www.stemoffaithministries.com or stemoffaithministries@gmail.com If you love to read my post and follow me on social media, click my page www.facebook.com/princemensahministries or whatapp me on +233548032145

If you have enjoyed my books and you want to promote them, please share the link to my Kindle book on Facebook and tell your friends. Many of your friends might decide to read my book when they see you post about it on Facebook.

Books authored by Prince Mensah

1. Am I called into ministry?
2. Practicing the prophetic
3. Fervent in spirit; serving the Lord
4. The Journey of the prophet
5. The Holy Spirit; my friend
6. Practical Ministry Training Manual
7. Practicing Deliverance Ministry
8. Am a Minstrel
9. Understanding the Healing fire
10. Understanding prophetic surge
11. Divine Prospects
12. Pneumaticos; riding the wind of the Holy Spirit
13. The Minister's Life
14. Ministerial Responsibilities

Need Mentorship From Prophet Prince Mensah?

Enroll now and be trained, equipped, imparted and activated for impactful ministry. We are mandated by the Lord to raise Mighty Warrior Ministers after God's heart.